Common Wetland Plants of Coastal California

A FIELD GUIDE FOR THE LAYMAN

Second Edition

Phyllis M. Faber

PICKLEWEED PRESS

PICKLEWEED PRESS
212 Del Casa
Mill Valley, California 94941

First Edition
First Printing 1982
Second Printing 1985
Third Printing 1990
Fourth Printing 1993

Second Edition
First Printing 1996

Printed in the United States of America

ISBN: 0-9607890-0-6
Library of Congress Catalogue Card Number: 81-86401

Other publications from Pickleweed Press:

Common Riparian Plants of California

ACKNOWLEDGMENTS

A number of people have helped in the preparation of this field guide — in its original form and its revised form. Wilma Follette and Gordon True (now deceased) made suggestions to make plant descriptions accurate, yet understandable, and both checked all plant identifications. Joy Zedler guided me to remnant salt marshes in southern California and Dan Ray from the North Coast Regional Coastal Commission to marshes around Humboldt Bay. Pat Stebbins (now deceased) of the State Coastal Commission provided maps and directions to several marshes along the coast. Tom Griggs from The Nature Conservancy provided specimens of the coastal variety of Orcutt's grass. Peter Baye reviewed name changes and made suggestions for the Second Edition. Joan Browning (now deceased) designed the original version of this field guide and Beth Hansen produced the new second edition. Eric Hammerling, a graduate student from the University of California, Berkeley revised Appendix 1: Definitions of Wetlands by State and Federal Agencies, to bring it up to date. I am deeply grateful to each of these people — friends and colleagues.

DEDICATION

This book is dedicated to those whose efforts promote the protection and preservation of the vital wetlands of California for present and future generations.

TABLE OF CONTENTS

PURPOSE OF THE FIELD GUIDE

The purpose of this field guide is to provide laymen with an easy method for identifying common wetland plants found in various wetland habitats in the coastal areas of California. Photocopy reproductions of the common plants are provided to provide a visual aid for easy identification of coastal wetland habitats. You can compare what you see in the field with a photocopy of the living plant shown in this book.

Precise delineation of wetlands is difficult. Boundaries are often obscured by filling, road building and other activities. Existing definitions and methods for wetland determination are often too technical for the average planner, developer or interested observer.

This field guide is intended to assist the layman in determining whether a site is a wetland or not by establishing the presence or absence of hydrophytic plants. The plants included in this manual are hydrophytes — plants tolerant of wet, or wet and salty conditions. Their presence indicates a wetland habitat.

Nearly 90 percent of California's wetland habitat has been destroyed by human activity over the past 150 years; the remaining fragments deserve full protection.

WHY WETLANDS MATTER

Beyond their obvious aesthetic and recreational value, wetlands play a vital role in the overall health of a coastal ecosystem. They produce an abundant yield of vegetation which, in turn, provides the basis for a complex food web nourishing a rich assortment of living organisms. They play a vital role in chemical and hydrologic cycles, and are sometimes described as "kidneys of the landscape." Without wetlands and the numerous funtions they perform, the quality of coastal life would be seriously diminished.

ABUNDANT PRODUCTIVITY

Plant productivity of wetlands is among the highest of the world's ecosystems. The capacity of an acre of coastal salt marsh to transform nutrients and water from soil, and carbon dioxide from air into plant tissue (photosynthesis) is twice that of an acre of corn or twenty times that of deep sea vegetation.

The abundant plant material of a wetland breaks down each winter. The flow of energy from the sun that begins with the growth of plants continues as plants die and decomposing bacteria surround and enrich fragmenting plant particles. These protein-rich particles form the base of a food web complex of larval and adult stages of invertebrates (amphipod, shrimp, crab, worm, mussel, clam, oyster, etc.) which, in turn, provide food for juvenile and adult stages of fish and flocks of shore birds and waterfowl. In turn, the fish and shellfish support a variety of marine mammals such as seal, otter and whales. As these animals die, they too, decompose and are recycled in the complex living web of wetland life.

In addition to providing food, wetlands provide shelter and resting grounds for a myriad of organisms. One has only to walk along the bayshore after a winter storm to see the number of migratory birds seeking shelter between storms or resting between tides.

ECOSYSTEM SERVICES

At the same time, wetlands perform an invaluable role of removing organic and inorganic nutrients and toxics from the system. Rainwater and storm runoff is cleansed where it travels through tidelands to the sea. Automotive and industrial pollutants are actively absorbed by a rich variety of microorganisms living in marsh soils and by mineral uptake of marsh vegetation.

Coastal wetlands also serve as a sediment trap for silt eroding from surrounding watersheds as well as markedly reducing shoreline erosion. Most important to developed areas within the coastal zone, wetlands absorb vast amounts of storm water, tidal or rainwater runoff. They serve as indespensible buffers between storm-driven waters and adjacent high ground.

AN ENDANGERED ECOSYSTEM

As critical as they are to the continuation of coastal life, California's wetlands have become one of the most endangered of the state's ecosystems. The combined loss of wetlands to agricultural use, for salt ponds and urban expansion (industrial, residential and recreational) has been nearly total in many coastal areas. Only fragments of former wetlands remain today. Our estuaries and coastal waters are impoverished and ecological services are limited when compared to a healthy wetland system.

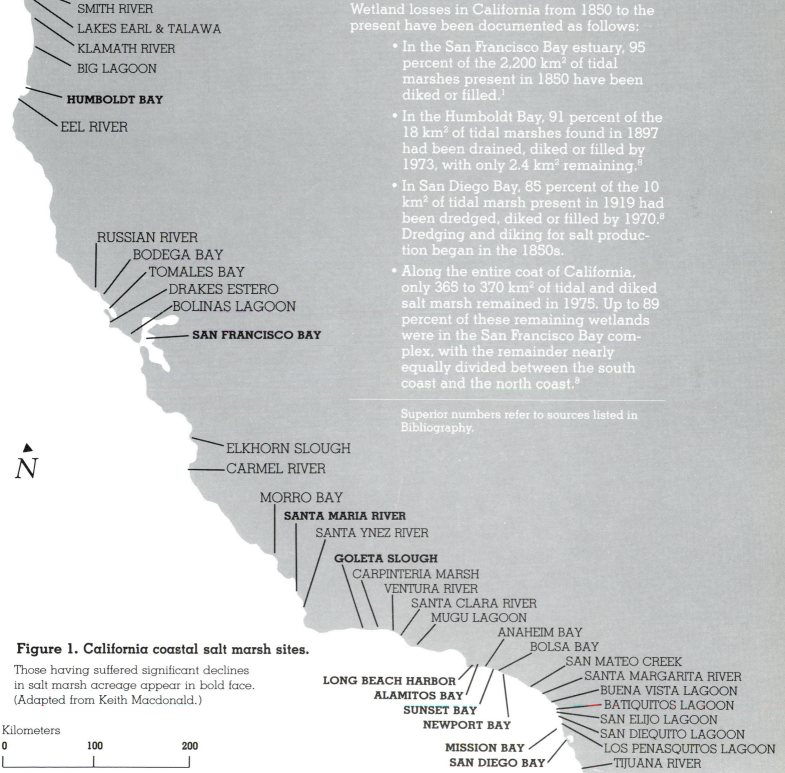

Wetland losses in California from 1850 to the present have been documented as follows:

- In the San Francisco Bay estuary, 95 percent of the 2,200 km² of tidal marshes present in 1850 have been diked or filled.[1]

- In the Humboldt Bay, 91 percent of the 18 km² of tidal marshes found in 1897 had been drained, diked or filled by 1973, with only 2.4 km² remaining.[8]

- In San Diego Bay, 85 percent of the 10 km² of tidal marsh present in 1919 had been dredged, diked or filled by 1970.[8] Dredging and diking for salt production began in the 1850s.

- Along the entire coat of California, only 365 to 370 km² of tidal and diked salt marsh remained in 1975. Up to 89 percent of these remaining wetlands were in the San Francisco Bay complex, with the remainder nearly equally divided between the south coast and the north coast.[8]

Superior numbers refer to sources listed in Bibliography.

SMITH RIVER
LAKES EARL & TALAWA
KLAMATH RIVER
BIG LAGOON

HUMBOLDT BAY

EEL RIVER

RUSSIAN RIVER
BODEGA BAY
TOMALES BAY
DRAKES ESTERO
BOLINAS LAGOON

SAN FRANCISCO BAY

N

ELKHORN SLOUGH
CARMEL RIVER

MORRO BAY
SANTA MARIA RIVER
SANTA YNEZ RIVER

GOLETA SLOUGH
CARPINTERIA MARSH
VENTURA RIVER
SANTA CLARA RIVER
MUGU LAGOON
ANAHEIM BAY
BOLSA BAY
SAN MATEO CREEK
LONG BEACH HARBOR
ALAMITOS BAY
SUNSET BAY
NEWPORT BAY
SANTA MARGARITA RIVER
BUENA VISTA LAGOON
BATIQUITOS LAGOON
SAN ELIJO LAGOON
SAN DIEQUITO LAGOON
MISSION BAY
LOS PENASQUITOS LAGOON
SAN DIEGO BAY
TIJUANA RIVER

Figure 1. California coastal salt marsh sites.

Those having suffered significant declines in salt marsh acreage appear in bold face. (Adapted from Keith Macdonald.)

Kilometers

0   100   200

THE PROBLEMS OF IDENTIFICATION

The ability to identify the various types of wetlands is not as simple as it might seem. Man-made disturbances over the last 130 years have added complexity to the problems naturally posed by the unique qualities and characteristics which differentiate wetlands from uplands. The key to the problem is the ability to identify characteristic plants.

Each habitat has its own peculiar characteristics. Plants are sensitive to a wide variety of physical factors, including:

- the length of time they are submerged by tide or by collected rainfall;

- soil conditions such as moisture, salinity, pH, organic content, nutrients, etc.;

- sedimentation and drainage patterns; evaporation and precipitation ratios; and microclimates.

The particular combination of physical factors at a given site will determine what plant species will grow. Certain plants may thrive in great profusion in one habitat but be scarce or non-existent in what appears to be a similar habitat. Each wetland is thus unique, supporting its own assemblage of plants determined by the physical factors of a particular site.

However, the boundaries between wetlands and uplands are easily blurred. In a typical salt marsh, the low and middle zones are relatively easily distinguished by a profusion of cordgrass at the water's edge, a vast expanse of picklewood in the middle zone and a band of salt grass at the upper edge of the marsh, the high zone. The presence of other salt-tolerant plants in the middle and high zones is determined by the special physical characteristics of the site. But in the upper zone of a marsh, man-made disturbances often have altered the elevations and drainage patterns, making the determination of the boundary with the upland difficult; in fact, it is often a job for the experts.

In addition, upland plants sometimes appear to grow in wetlands, and vice-versa. For example, salt grass can be found in the spray zone of coastal bluffs, or brass buttons may be found at inland sites of rainwater ponding or in diked areas containing high levels of residual salts. Definitions of wetlands by various state and federal agencies are found in Appendix 1.

INDICATOR PLANTS ARE THE KEY TO IDENTIFICATION

While experts will want to consider soil types in addition to plant associations, laymen often can make accurate identifications of wetland habitats by looking for plants which are characteristic, or indicative, of particular wetlands.

If two or three of the plants found in this field guide are discovered within a radius of five or six feet, it is probable that the site is a wetland habitat. If only one of the plants in the guidebook is found in the upper marsh, the area **may be** a wetland, particularly if there is a good-sized patch of a plant such as *Frankenia*. But if there are no plants matching those in the field guide the area is **probably not** a wetland.

The exception to these rules lies in identification of plants characteristic of vernal pools. Such identification is complicated by the fact that once the pools have dried up following winter rains, vegetation also dries and cannot be found until the following year when seeds germinate and plants return with a new winter supply of moisture. Thus, the apparent absence of indicator plants in a suspected vernal pool in the summer or fall does not rule out the possibility that the area is a vernal pool.

HOW TO USE THE FIELD GUIDE

The organization, illustrations and descriptions in this guidebook are intended to make it as easy as possible for the layman to identify California wetlands through the identification of common plants unique to each wetland habitat type.

Illustrations are photocopies of actual plants. Plants in the field may be somewhat smaller or larger depending on growth conditions at a particular site. For example, a plant growing around San Francisco Bay may grow to a height of six inches, while the same species growing in Humboldt Bay, with its greater annual rainfall, may attain a height of ten inches. Much of the overall form and gestalt of the plant is retained in the photocopy process; however, floral details used by botanists to identify plants are lost. The guidebook is not intended to be used other than as a general tool in the identification of common wetland plants.

Plants have been separated into five habitat types:

Each section has a brief introduction to a habitat type, followed by individual plant illustrations. Accompanying descriptions include common and botanical names, distribution and range, plant form and size, leaf and floral forms and bloom times.

When you are in the field, look at the plants around you and compare them to the illustration in the five habitat sections listed below. If your plant is not included in the section where you expect it to be, for example in a salt marsh, look in the adjacent section. Fresh-water often mixes with salt so that salt marshes merge into brackish marshes and brackish marshes merge into fresh-water marshes.

Salt marsh plants are found along the coast or in portions of a bay where tidal waters are largely saline.

Brackish marsh plants are found where there is a mix of fresh and salt water. For example, where streams drain into a salt marsh or fresh riverine water mixes with saline tidal waters, a flora occurs that is tolerant to these conditions.

Fresh-water marsh plants are found where water is fresh and generally still, such as a river backwater, a lake or pond.

Riparian plants are found beside a river or stream.

Vernal Pool plants are found in winter or early spring where there are drying ponds or puddles. These pools may be found on coastal terraces or bluff tops at considerable distances from a shoreline. In late spring, summer and fall, when water has evaporated and plants have dried and gone to seed, vernal pools are hard to locate and vegetation is difficult to identify. It is best to wait for spring!

ABOUT PLANT NAMES: COMMON AND SCIENTIFIC

Many plants have common names; more of them do not. Some plants have more than one common name. For example, pickleweed is also known as glasswort, marsh samphire, saltwort and chicken toe in different parts of the country. Generally accepted common names are given in each plant description.

All plants have a single accepted genus and species name assigned by one author. Names are sometimes changed according to an internationally accepted convention by work of later investigators; however, there is always only one name universally recognized. Botanical names used in this edition are consistent with those found in *The Jepson Manual of Higher Plants* (1993), the most recently published authority.

Habitat, range and descriptive information has been derived from *The Jepson Manual* (1993), *A California Flora* by Munz and Keck (1973), and *A Flora of the Marshes of California* by Mason (1957). Anyone wishing to go beyond the information provided in this field guide may wish to consult these comprehensive books about the flora of California and particularly Mason for his exhaustive description of the flora of California marshes which includes excellent drawings of many of the plants. Amateurs and professionals alike rely on these books.

ABOUT

Salt Marshes

The coastal salt marsh community is found throughout coastal California in estuaries, bays, and other areas that are somewhat protected from open coastal winds and waves.

Marshes border the mudflat community, a rich community of algae, diatoms and invertebrates, which is generally found between mean low water and mean sea level. Salt marshes are distinguished from mudflats by the presence of upright herbaceous vegetation, which colonizes mudflats at about mean sea level and extends up into the extreme high-tide line. The major tidal marshes along the California coast are found in Humboldt Bay, San Francisco Bay, Tomales Bay, Drake's Estero, Elkhorn Slough, Morro Bay, Mugu Lagoon, Bolsa Chica Bay, the lagoons of Southern California, Mission Bay in San Diego and the Tijuana River delta.

Different vegetational zones occur as a result of a limited tolerance that each plant species has for the harsh conditions found in a marsh. The physical factors limiting the plants include: tidal inundations of salt or brackish water (sea water contains 3.5 percent salt); water-saturated soils containing few air spaces and hence reduced oxygen levels; and an environment fully exposed to sun, wide temperature fluctuations and wind.

The lowest zones of a west coast salt marsh are inundated twice daily while the upper zones may be inundated only once or twice a month, or even by only the highest spring tides as shown in Figure 2. Of the thousands of plant species in North America, only cordgrass, *Spartina foliosa*, thrives in the lowest zone of a salt marsh (approximately from mean sea level to mean high tide). Curiously, this plant is missing from salt marshes south of San Francisco to Point Conception.

The middle zone (approximately from mean high tide to mean higher high tide) is characterized by pickleweed, *Salicornia sp.*, which is less tolerant of tidal inundation. Perennial pickleweed (*Salicornia virginica*) is the dominant plant of California marshes.

The upper zone (approximately from mean higher high tide to the extreme high tide line) is dominated by salt grass (*Distichlis spicata*) which tolerates only occasional tidal inundation.

The zonation of the marshes of Southern California (Mugu Lagoon, Anaheim Bay, Newport Bay, Mission Bay, San Diego Bay and the Tijuana River Estuary) is somewhat more complex. A zone of saltwort (*Batis maritima*,) and an annual pickleweed (*Salicornia bigelovi*) intergrades with cordgrass in the low zone and with perennial pickleweed and other middle zone species at higher elevations.

salt grass
MHHT - EHT
+6' — +8'

pickleweed
MHT - MHHT
+4' — +6'

cordgrass
MSL - MHT
0 — +4'

mudflat

Figure 2. Profile of a typical west coast salt marsh
MSL = mean sea level, MHT = mean high tide. MHHT = mean higher high tide, EHT = extreme high tide

SPECIAL CHARACTERISTICS OF SALT MARSH PLANTS:

- hollow passages from leaves to roots for air movement
- oxidation of surrounding mud
- reversal of osmotic flow by salt concentration
- excretion of salt by glands on leaves and stems

All plants that live in the low zones of a wetland, where there is standing water for large portions of a tidal cycle, have special adaptations which enable them to thrive where other plants would die.

To begin with, **air diffuses through hollow tubes** connecting stomata (openings on leaf surfaces) with hollow spaces in the roots, thus supplying oxygen which is essential to the health of root cells.

In addition, **air diffuses through root cell walls into surrounding mud.** In the mud, the air oxidizes a form of iron sulfide, changing it to a rust-colored iron oxide and ferrous sulfate. These are soluble and usable nutrients, particularly essential to cordgrass with its unusually high requirements for iron. This area of light brown oxygenated mud immediately surrounding the fine roots is easily distinguishable from the blackish-gray, anaerobic mud typically found throughout a marsh.

To survive the desert-like environment of a salt marsh (salty soils and a lack of fresh water), all salt-tolerant plants, known as halophytes, have an adaptation that enables then to **reverse the osmotic flow of water.** They are able to concentrate salt ions in root cells to levels higher than sea water, thus assuring a flow of water into the plant from the surrounding salty mud. In the normal process of osmosis, water flows across a membrane from a lower concentration of salt toward a higher concentration. In other words, water would flow away from a plant with normally low salt concentrations in root tissues into the surrounding salty soils, making the environment physiologically uninhabitable for plant life. By reversing this process, halophytes can thrive where other species cannot live.

Unfortunately for the plant, the same salt, concentrated in the roots, can interfere with enzymatic processes in stem and leaf cell metabolism. This requires another adaptation, one that cordgrass shares with other halophytes; **an ability to excrete salt by special glands found along stems and leaf surfaces.** Careful inspection will reveal excreted salt crystals on the leaves of a variety of marsh plants, including cordgrass, salt grass, and marsh rosemary. Using a totally different approach, pickleweed eliminates salt by isolating it in "joints," or modified reduced leaves and stems. In the fall, these terminal compartments turn pink or red, giving marshes a soft rosy hue before the joints dry up and break off after winter rains, carrying away stored salt with plant tissues.

GROWING UP IN A SALT MARSH

Salt marshes expand into mudflat areas when silt-laden waters, slowed by the stands of cordgrass, deposit silt at the land/water interface. These deposits increase marsh plain elevations until they become suitable for cordgrass colonization.

Cordgrass spreads principally from new plants sprouting from rhizomes (underground stems). Newly colonized areas often occur at the edge of a bay or in meanders. In new areas of marsh such as behind newly-opened dikes, cordgrass appears to be colonized initially by seed. Once established, expansion occurs by means of vegetative growth of rhizomes. The establishment of seeds appears to be limited by competition from already established plants.

On the other hand, pickleweed reproduces principally by seed. In order for seeds to germinate, soil salinity must drop from around six percent, which is tolerable for adult plants in a typical marsh, to two to three percent following the winter rains. Heavy winter rains thus appear to produce good pickleweed years in a salt marsh.

FRANKENIA FAMILY *Frankeniaceae*

Alkali Heath

Frankenia salina

- Common in upper salt marshes from Central California to Mexico
- Low, bushy perennial often growing in large patches; 6 to 12 inches tall
- Small, opposite, oval leaves in bundles
- Small, pink-petaled flowers, solitary in leaf axils or clustered on small branches; blooms June-October

MUSTARD FAMILY *Brassicaceae*

- An aggressive invader of disturbed upland margins of coastal salt marshes and saline shorelines
- An erect grayish perennial that spreads widely from underground root system; 16-40 inches tall

Peppergrass

Lepidium latifolium

- Slightly toothed to entire leaves; $1/3$-$1\,1/2$ inches wide
- Large many-flowered inflorescence, tiny white petals; seeds a flattened unwinged elipse; blooms June-August

PINK FAMILY *Caryophyllaceae*

Sand Spurrey

Spergularia macrotheca

- Common on edges of upper zone of coastal saltmarshes, salt flats, coastal bluffs throughout California
- Much-branched, matted growth; 2 to 12 inches
- Small, linear leaves
- Tiny, white-to-pink flowers; blooms March-September

FIG-MARIGOLD FAMILY *Azoaceae*

- Upper edge of disturbed coastal salt marshes and bluffs from Monterey south
- Much branched, trailing, prostrate annual or biennial; 8-24 inches long
- Leaves succulent with shining vescicles, flat and ovate; 3/4 to 4 inches long

Crystalline Iceplant

Mesembryanthemum crystallinum

- Showy flowers with many linear petals, white fading to pink; blooms March-October
- *M. nodiflorum* is common in S.F. Bay on saline levees

GOOSEFOOT FAMILY *Chenopodiaceae*

Fat Hen, Saltbush

Atriplex triangularis

- Common in upper zone of salt marshes throughout coastal California
- Simple to much-branched annual; 12 to 40 inches tall
- Broadly triangular, green leaves
- Small, greenish flowers without petals; blooms June-November

GOOSEFOOT FAMILY *Chenopodiaceae*

Australian Saltbush

Atriplex semibaccata

- Abundant in upper zone and along edges of many coastal salt marshes from Central to Southern California
- Prostrate, much-branched, mat-forming perennial; 8 to 45 inches tall
- Many, small, grey-scurfy to greenish, elliptic to oblong, irregularly toothed leaves
- Small, inconspicuous, green flowers; fruiting bracts become red and fleshy; blooms April-December

GOOSEFOOT FAMILY *Chenopodiaceae*

Goosefoot

Chenopodium macrospermum
var. *farinosum*

- Wet places, high ponded water on dunes, reservoirs, and marshes; Orange to Humboldt counties
- Branched annual with upper stems ascending; 4-20 inches tall
- Thick to fleshy triangular leaves; some densely powdery
- Dense spikes in axils of upper leaves; blooms July-October

GOOSEFOOT FAMILY *Chenopodiaceae*

Pickleweed, Glasswort

Salicornia subterminalis

- Occasional in middle zone of coastal marshes from San Francisco Bay to Southern California
- Perennial with stems widely spreading or erect and compact; 6 to 12 inches
- Branchlets many; leaves reduced to succulent joints
- Flower-bearing scales; blooms April-September

GOOSEFOOT FAMILY *Chenopodiaceae*

Common Pickleweed

Salicornia virginica

- Abundant perennial, forming extensive colonies in middle zone of coastal salt marshes throughout coastal California
- Erect or spreading growth; 8 to 25 inches tall
- Leaves reduced to succulent joints
- Flower-bearing scales; blooms April-September

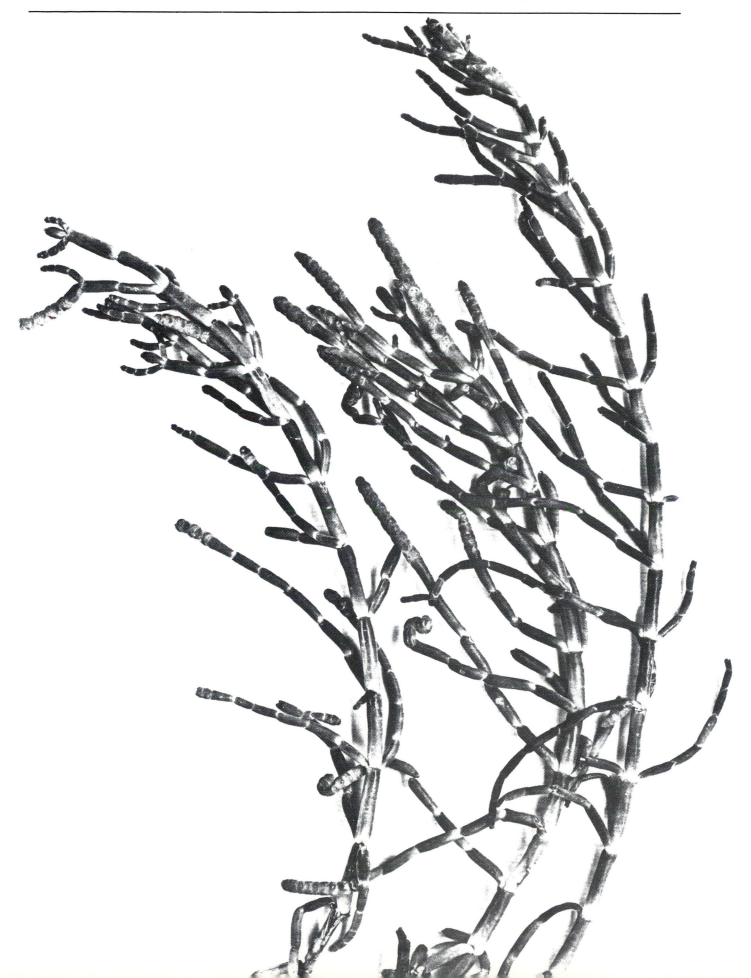

GOOSEFOOT FAMILY *Chenopodiaceae*

Pickleweed

Salicornia bigelovii

- Occasional in middle zone of coastal salt marshes from Los Angeles County into Mexico, often growing in association with Batis
- Erect annual, simple-stemmed or with strongly ascending branches; 4 to 20 inches tall
- Leaves reduced to succulent joints
- Flower-bearing scales; blooms July-November

GOOSEFOOT FAMILY *Chenopodiaceae*

Pickleweed

Salicornia europea*

- Occasional in middle zone of coastal salt marshes in San Diego, Point Mugu and San Francisco Bay
- Low, densely bushy annual, branched from base; 4 to 8 inches tall
- Leaves reduced to succulent joints
- Flower-bearing scales; blooms July-November

* Mason separates *S. europaea* into *S. rubra* (S.F. Bay) and *S. depressa* (S.F. Bay and San Diego)

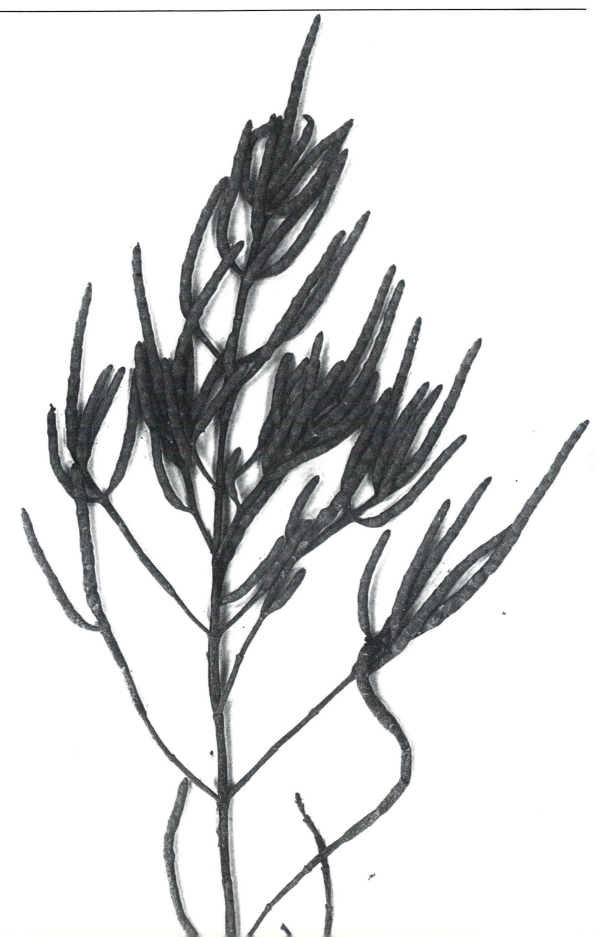

GOOSEFOOT FAMILY *Chenopodiaceae*

Russian Thistle

Salsola soda

- Invasive non-native plant in coastal salt marshes, particularly San Francisco Bay
- Simple to much branched annual; 6-17 inches tall
- Reduced, thick-ridged and spine tipped leaves
- Inconspicuous flowers with winged sepals and short-tubercled fruit in axils; blooms July-October

GOOSEFOOT FAMILY *Chenopodiaceae*

Sea-Blite

Suaeda californica

- Common in upper salt marsh from Central to Southern California
- Much-branched perennial, erect or spreading; 12 to 32 inches
- Alternate, narrow, linear leaves crowded on stem
- Small, greenish flowers with no petals; blooms July-October

GOOSEFOOT FAMILY *Chenopodiaceae*

Sea-Blite

Suaeda fruticosa

- Occasional in upper zone of coastal salt marshes in Southern California
- Much-branched perennial; 8 to 30 inches
- Many, narrow, linear, succulent leaves; ½-¾ inch long
- Inconspicuous greenish flowers without petals, clustered in axils of uppermost leaves and giving the appearance of a spike; blooms July-October

BATIS FAMILY *Batidaceae*

Saltwort

Batis maritima

- Common in coastal salt marshes from Los Angeles County into Mexico
- Erect or prostrate perennial; 4 to 40 inches long
- Long, narrow, succulent leaves
- Separate male and female flowers, both inconspicuous and found in axils of leaves; blooms July-October

PRIMROSE FAMILY *Primulaceae*

Sea-Milkwort

Glaux maritima

- Middle zone of coastal salt marshes from San Luis Obispo County to Humboldt County
- Low, fleshy perennial with branched slender stems
- Fleshy, opposite, sessile leaves
- Inconspicuous, minute, white-to-reddish flowers in leaf axils; blooms May-July

LEADWORT FAMILY *Plumbaginaceae*

Marsh Rosemary

Limonium californicum

- Occasional in upper zone of salt marshes throughout coastal California
- Erect, woody perennial; 8 to 20 inches tall
- Broad, flat, basal leaves often covered with excreted salt crystals
- Pale, violet flowers crowding branched spikes; blooms July-December

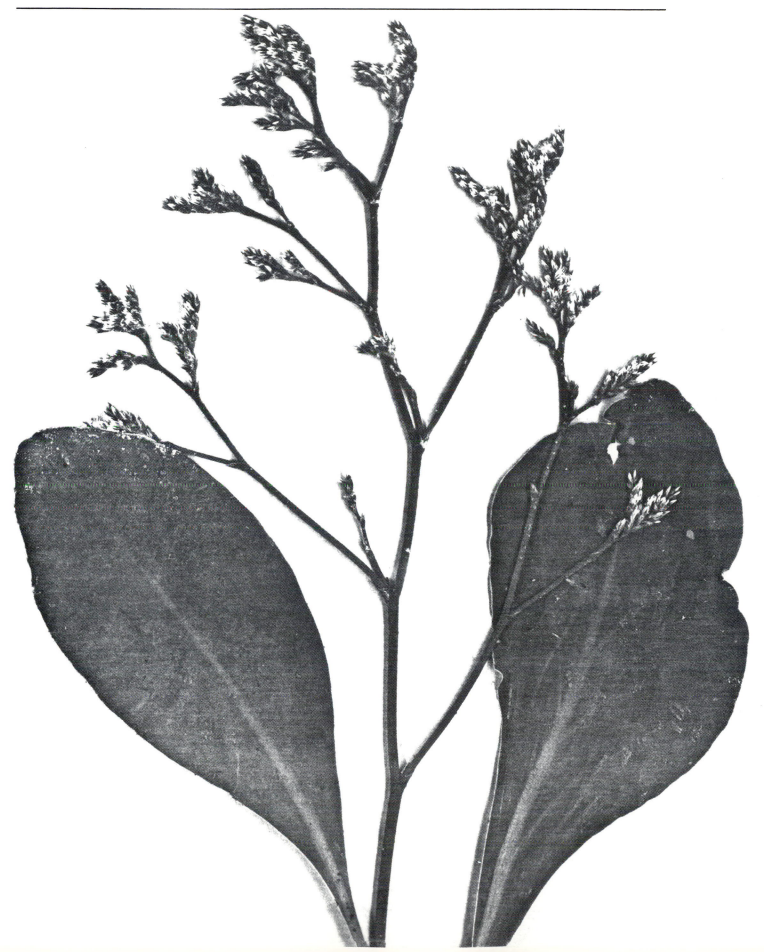

MORNING-GLORY FAMILY *Convolvulaceae*

Dodder

Cuscuta salina

- Occasional parasite on plants of middle and upper zone of salt marshes throughout coastal California
- Slender orange twining stems, often forming dense mats which fade when the plant begins to flower
- Leaves reduced to minutes scales
- Small, waxy-white flowers; blooms May-September

MORNING-GLORY FAMILY *Convolvulaceae*

Alkali Weed

Cressa truxillensis

- Upper zone and bordering salt marshes throughout coastal California
- Low much-branched perennial; 4 to 8 inches tall
- Small, woolly, gray, alternate leaves
- Small, white flowers in leaf axils; blooms May-October

BORAGE FAMILY *Boraginaceae*

Seaside Heliotrope

Heliotropium curassavicum var. oculatum

- Marshes, stream beds, and alkaline flats throughout coastal California
- Perennial with diffusely branching stems; 4 to 20 inches tall
- Succulent, smooth, linear to spatula-like leaves
- Small, white flowers with yellow spots in throat, purpling with age and growing on an uncoiling inflorescence; blooms March-October

FIGWORT FAMILY *Scrophulariaceae*

Johnny-nip

Castilleja ambigua

- Salt marshes near the coast, central coast to Br. Columbia
- Much-branched decumbent annual; 4 to 10 inches tall
- Narrow lance-shaped alternate leaves; $^1/_{10}$ to $^2/_{10}$ inches
- Short dense flower spikes, bracts white or yellowish
- Closely related to three species of salt marsh bird's beak *Cordylanthus* spp., all rare because of major coastal salt marsh habitat loss.

SUNFLOWER FAMILY *Asteraceae*

Jaumea

Jaumea carnosa

- Common in middle zone of scattered salt marshes throughout coastal California
- Spreading, prostrate perennial often growing in sizable patches; 4 to 12 inches
- Narrow, fleshy leaves
- Yellow, compound inflorescence in a fairly inconspicuous head; blooms May-October

SUNFLOWER FAMILY *Asteraceae*

Marsh Gum-plant

Grindelia stricta var. *angustifolia*

- Common in upper marsh of San Francisco, San Pablo, and Suisun bays
- Erect perennial; up to 60 inches tall
- Thickish leaves
- Resinous, gummy buds developing into showy, bright-yellow flowers; blooms August-October

SUNFLOWER FAMILY *Asteraceae*

Gum-Plant

Grindelia stricta

- Common in upper zone of coastal salt marshes from Southern California north into Oregon
- Erect perennial; 12 to 16 inches tall
- Thickish leaves
- Resinous, gummy buds developing into showy, bright-yellow flowers; blooms June-September

SUNFLOWER FAMILY *Asteraceae*

Brass Buttons

Cotula coronopifolia

- Common on mud and moist banks particularly in salt marshes throughout coastal California
- Low, branched, decumbent perennials; 8 to 12 inches
- Long, fleshy leaves, sometimes coarse and deeply toothed
- Bright-yellow, button-like, compound inflorescence lacking ray flowers; blooms March-December

SUNFLOWER FAMILY *Asteraceae*

Salt Marsh Fleabane

Pluchea purpurascens

- Occasional in salt marshes and alkaline, wet places from San Francisco Bay to Southern California
- Annual, erect, branching plant; 1 to 3 feet tall
- Oval, pointed, glandular, toothed leaves
- Large clusters of smallish, reddish-purple flowers; blooms July-November

ARROWGRASS FAMILY *Juncaginaceae*

Arrowgrass

Triglochin concinna

- Occasional in salt marshes, seeps and mudflats along coast
- Slender plants growing from rhizomes, less than 8 inches tall
- Fleshy roundish stem-like leaves sheathing at their base
- Inconspicuous greenish flowers on a long-stemmed leafless flower spike; blooms March-August

ARROWGRASS FAMILY *Juncaginaceae*

Sea Arrowgrass

*Triglochin maritima**

- Occasional in salt marshes, alkaline flats and boggy places from San Francisco Bay north in coastal California
- Coarse or slender plant growing in dense clumps; 10 to 25 inches high
- Fleshy, long, roundish stem-like leaves which are sheathing at base
- Inconspicuous greenish or reddish flowers on a long-stemmed leafless flower spike; blooms April-August

* Two smaller forms, *T.concinna* and *T. striata*, are also found in coastal salt marshes

GRASS FAMILY *Poaceae*

Saltgrass

Distichlis spicata

- Abundant in upper zone of salt marshes throughout coastal California
- Low perennial, often prostrate; 8 to 12 inches tall
- Stiff, wiry, green leaves
- Flowers on densely arranged spike with male and female inflorescences located on separate plants; blooms April-July

GRASS FAMILY *Poaceae*

Hainardia

*Hainardia cylindrica
(Monerma cylindrica)*

- Occasional in disturbed well drained soils of coastal salt marshes
- Ascending to erect, slender, branched annual grass; 8-20 inches tall
- Leaf blade generally flat, ribbed and narrow
- Inflorescence cylindric, stiff, and straight; 4-8 inches long; blooms May-July

GRASS FAMILY *Poaceae*

Shoregrass

Monanthochloe littoralis

- Common in upper zone of salt marshes and tidal flats from Santa Barbara County into Mexico
- Low, extensively creeping perennial grass with short, erect branches; 4 to 11 inches tall
- Leaf blades sickle-shaped, giving appearance of clusters
- Short spikelets of inconspicuous flowers nearly concealed in leaves; blooms May-June

GRASS FAMILY *Poaceae*

Sicklegrass

Parapholis incurva

- Occasional in disturbed well drained soils of coastal salt marshes
- Decumbent to erect, sometimes branching annual grass; 1.5 to 14 inches tall
- Leaf blade flat, somewhat inrolled and ribbed; $\frac{1}{10}$ to $\frac{1}{8}$ inches wide
- Inflorescence a curved twisted spike; 1 to 6 inches long; blooms April-June

GRASS FAMILY *Poaceae*

Dense-flowered Cordgrass

Spartina densiflora

- Common in salt marshes in Humboldt Bay and newly escaped into San Francisco Bay in Marin County
- Erect perennial grass which grows in dense clumps; 1-4 feet tall
- Long, tough, greyish leaves; ¼ to ⅓ inch wide.
- Inflorescence a 5-6 inch spike with dense colorless flowers, blooms July-November
- In the 1970s, the common east coast salt-water cordgrass (*Spartina alterniflora*) was introduced to San Francisco Bay where it has spread aggressively, particularly in South and East Bay marshes. It is tall (3-7 feet), more robust and grows at lower elevations than the native cordgrass, *S. foliosa*.

GRASS FAMILY *Poaceae*

Cordgrass

Spartina foliosa

- Common in lowest zone of many salt marshes throughout coastal California
- Erect, perennial grass which spreads vegetatively; 1-4 feet tall
- Long, tough leaves; ⅓ to ½ inch wide.
- Inflorescence a 5-6 inch spike with dense, colorless flowers; blooms July-November

ABOUT

Brackish Marshes

Brackish marshes are found where fresh water mixes with salt water. Some of the best examples are found in the San Francisco Bay estuary, in particular in San Pablo Bay where run-off from the Sierra flows into the bay from the Sacramento and San Joaquin rivers. The marshes in Suisun Bay and the lower delta were once natural brackish marshes, but they have been diked and modified to provide waterfowl habitat and agricultural lands. Plants typical of brackish marshes often can be found in drainage sloughs and where fresh-water drainages enter a salt marsh. A fine example of the latter can be found at China Camp State Park in Marin County.

A brackish marsh in one of the most restrictive habitat types because of the fluctuations of fresh and salt water. During the winter and spring season of heavy rains and stream runoff, marshes may be flooded for long periods by fresh water, while in the summer and fall, salty tidal waters may predominate. Few species of plants can tolerate large ranges of salinity and long periods of submergence.

Pure stands of bulrush, *Scirpus acutus*, grow in deep water and are succeeded by cattails, *Thypha* sp., growing in solid stands higher up on the banks. Other species of scirpus, *S. americanus* and *S. robustus*, are found with the cattails, often in large unmixed stands. Boundaries between salt and brackish marshes fluctuate as seasonal rainfall fluctuates.

SPECIAL CHARACTERISTICS OF BRACKISH MARSH PLANTS

- hollow passages from leaves to roots for air diffusion
- reverse osmotic flow from soil to plant roots by salt concentration in roots
- small root and stout rhizome systems

Brackish plants have the same adaptations as salt marsh plants. They have hollow passages in their leaves and stems enabling air to move to the roots freely. They can cope with a degree of salt in their environment by concentrating salt in root cells.

Because of the ready availability of water, root systems tend to be small; however, rhizomes (underground stems) from which new plants emerge are stout and grow on or just under the surface of the mud. Emerging plants become interlaced and dense resulting in the formation of a silt and debris trap and a rapid buildup of the marsh margin.

PLANTAIN FAMILY *Plantaginaceae*

Plantain

*Plantago hirtella
var. galeottiana**

- Occasional in salt marshes and moist banks throughout coastal California
- Low growing perennial with a hairy flower stalk; 4 to 10 inches tall
- Oval, pointed leaves with prominent veins
- Tiny, membranaceous flowers on a dense, cylindric spike; blooms May–September

* *P. major var. scopulorum* and *P. coronopus* are also commonly found in coastal wetlands

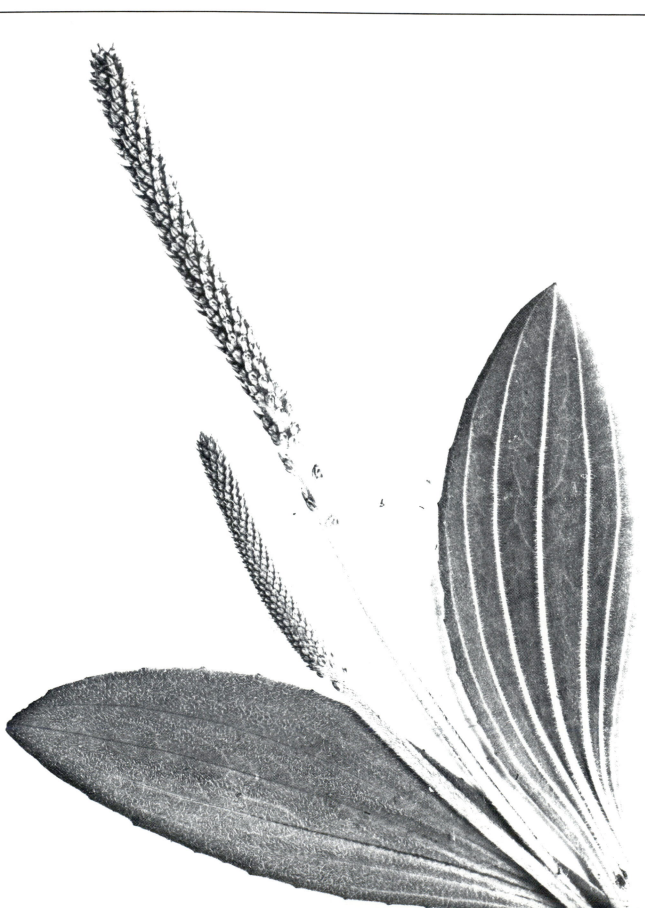

CARROT FAMILY *Apiaceae*

Lilaeopsis

Lilaeopsis occidentalis

- Occasional in salt marshes and brackish flats from Marin and Solano Counties north in coastal California
- Small, low, tufted perennial; 1 to 6 inches tall
- Leaves reduced to hollow, round, leaf-like structures (phyllodes), with observable cross-wall partitions
- Tiny, white flowers in umbels located in leaf axils; blooms June-August

WATER-PLANTAIN FAMILY *Alismataceae*

- Occasional on margins of ponds and shores of brackish and freshwater marshes from Ventura County north in coastal California
- Erect perennial in shallow water or wet mud; 4 to 45 inches tall
- Leaves have large, distinctive, ovoid leaf blades that taper to a point and emerge from the ground in a clump
- Fragile white to pinkish flowers on whorled flowering branches of an inflorescence taller than the leaves; blooms June-July

Water-Plantain

Alisma triviale

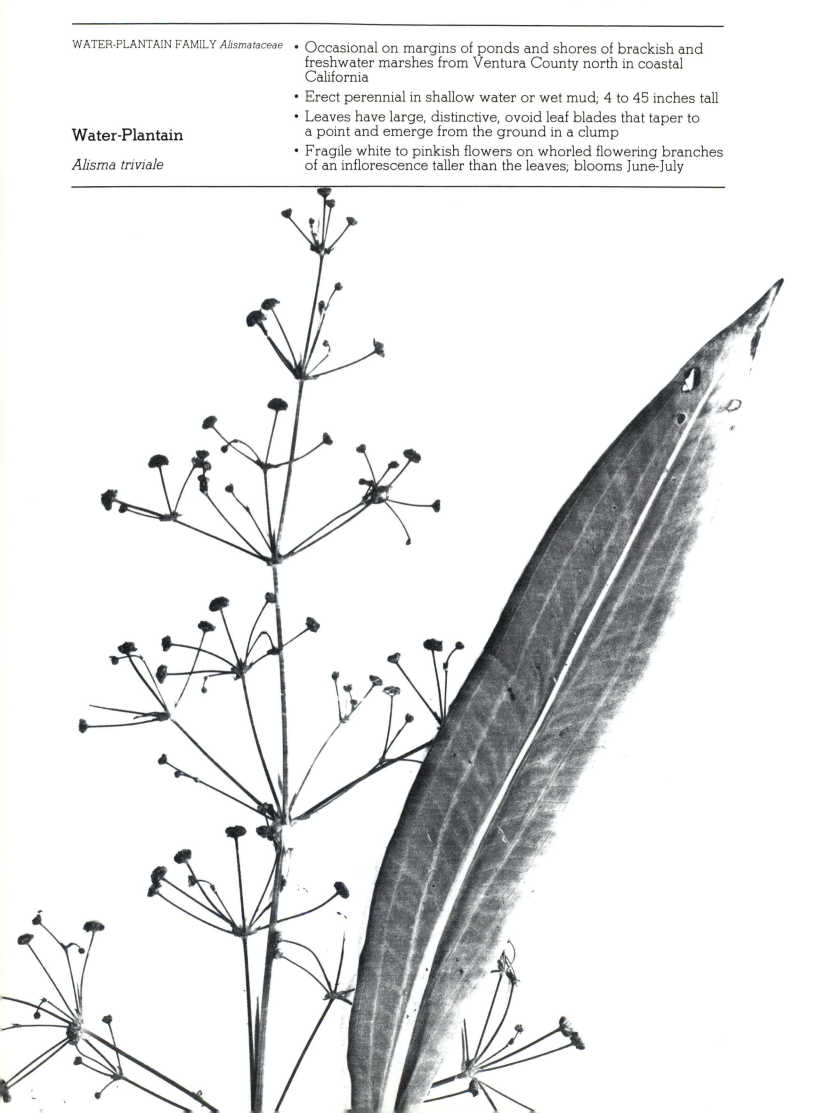

DITCH-GRASS FAMILY *Ruppiaceae*

Ditch-Grass

Ruppia maritima

- Aquatic plants of brackish ponds or marshes throughout coastal California
- Much-branched plant; 2 to 20 feet long
- Threadlike leaves
- Inconspicuous flowers in an enclosing sheath borne on elongated straight flower stalk; blooms April-July

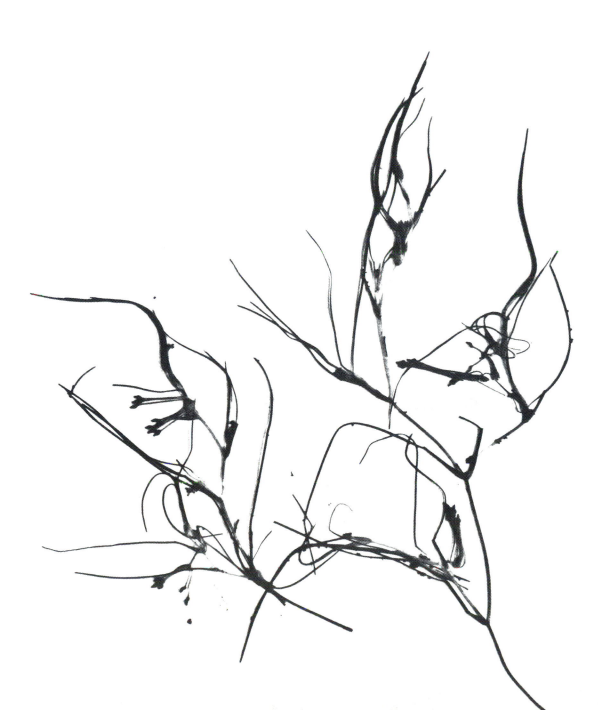

RUSH FAMILY *Juncaceae*

- Marshes and boggy moist places near the coast from Santa Barbara County north to Oregon
- Wiry, erect perennial, with bright-green stems growing in tufts; 1.5 to 4 feet tall
- Round, stiff stems; pale, loose leaf-sheaths
- Lateral inflorescence a many-flowered congested panicle; blooms June-July

* *Juncus patens* often grows with this plant and can be distinguished by its blue-green appearance.

Common Rush

Juncus effusus var. brunneus* †

† The genus *Juncus*, commonly called Rush or Wire Grass, is a large group of over 200 species distributed world-wide, with 49 species found throughout California and 21 in coastal California. Rushes are usually found in moist places growing with grasses and sedges.

RUSH FAMILY *Juncaceae*

- Common and widespread in wet ground throughout coastal California
- Erect, round, wiry-stemmed perennial growing from creeping rootstock, singly or in clumps; 8 to 30 inches tall
- Rudimentary leaf consisting of basal sheath
- Tiny, purplish-brown flowers with greenish centers; blooms May–August

Rush

*Juncus balticus**

* The genus *Juncus*, commonly called Rush or Wire Grass, is a large group of over 200 species distributed world-wide, with 49 species found throughout California and 21 in coastal California. Rushes are usually found in moist places growing with grasses and sedges.

RUSH FAMILY *Juncaceae*

- Widely distributed along streams or in dried pools throughout coastal California
- Annual, branching at base; 3 to 8 inches tall
- Narrow bristly leaves
- Flowers in uncoiling, spike-like clusters with green to brownish or purplish petals; blooms May-July

Toad Rush

Juncus bufonius*

* The genus *Juncus*, commonly called Rush or Wire Grass, is a large group of over 200 species distributed world-wide, with 49 species found throughout California and 21 in coastal California. Rushes are usually found in moist places growing with grasses and sedges.

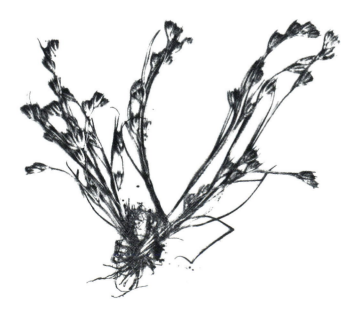

SEDGE FAMILY *Cyperaceae*

- Common in salt, freshwater or alkaline marshes throughout coastal California
- Perennial sedge with sharply triangular stems; 1.5 to 4.5 feet tall
- One or more stem leaves, typically ¼ inch wide, but sometimes up to ¾ inch; 2-5 unequal, short leaves clustered just below inflorescence.
- Inflorescence capitate with several tightly-clustered, ovate, reddish-brown spikelets; blooms April-August

* The genus *Scirpus*, commonly called Bulrush or Tule, is in the Sedge family and is a large genus of over 200 species distributed world-wide with 17 species found throughout California and 9 in coastal California.

Alkali Bulrush

Scirpus maritimus*

SEDGE FAMILY *Cyperaceae*

Three Square

*Scirpus americanus**

- Widely distributed in wet ground throughout coastal California
- Perennial with sharply triangular, stiff stems; 1 to 3.5 feet tall
- Narrow, keeled leaves, 6 inches long, with a solitary leaf growing beyond the inflorescence
- Inflorescence a capitate cluster of 1 to 7 pale to chocolate— brown spikelets; blooms May-August

* The genus *Scirpus*, commonly called Bulrush or Tule, is in the Sedge family and is a large genus of over 200 species distributed world-wide with 17 species found throughout California and 9 in coastal California.

SEDGE FAMILY *Cyperaceae*

Olney's Bulrush

Scirpus americanus (Scirpus olneyi*)

- Widespread in brackish and freshwater marshes throughout coastal California
- Perennial with stout, sharply triangular, concave-sided stems; 1.5 to 7 feet tall
- Short erect leaf blades growing beyond the inflorescence
- A head-like cluster of inconspicuous, scale-like, brown flowers just below the tip of the stem; blooms June to August

* Though this species has been submerged into *S. americanus* in the 1993 *Jepson Manual*, it appears to be distinct in many locations.

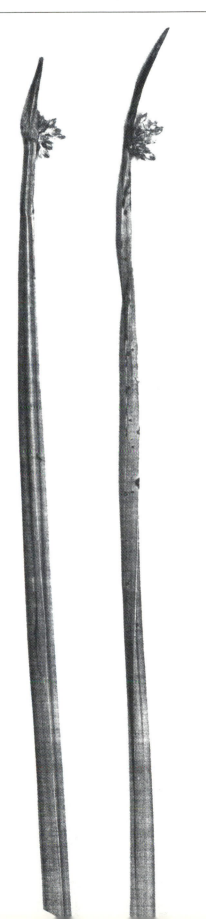

SEDGE FAMILY *Cyperaceae*

- Abundant in brackish and freshwater marshes throughout coastal California
- Perennial with round, stout stems; up to 15 feet
- Leaves reduced to basal sheaths except a solitary, round leaf, shorter than the inflorescence but appearing as a continuation of the stem
- Inflorescence a dense to somewhat dense, capitate cluster of pale-brown to reddish-brown spikelets; blooms May-August

* The genus *Scirpus*, commonly called Bulrush or Tule, is in the Sedge family and is a large genus of over 200 species distributed world-wide with 17 species found throughout California and 9 in coastal California.

Common Tule

*Scirpus acutus**

SEDGE FAMILY *Cyperaceae*

- Common in brackish marshes along the coast from San Diego County to Marin and Napa counties
- Perennial sedge with stout, roundish to triangular stems; up to 13 feet tall
- Leaves reduced to basal sheaths except a solitary, erect leaf, shorter than the inflorescence
- Inflorescence a loose arrangement of narrow, reddish-brown spikelets; blooms June-September

* The genus *Scirpus*, commonly called Bulrush or Tule, is in the Sedge family and is a large genus of over 200 species distributed world-wide with 17 species found throughout California and 9 in coastal California.

California Bulrush

Scirpus californicus*

GRASS FAMILY *Poaceae*

Common Reed

Phragmites australis

- Occasional in freshwater marshes or along stream banks throughout coastal California
- A robust, weedy perennial grass forming cane-like thickets in wet places; 6 to 12 feet tall
- Broad-leafed stems arising from creeping rhizomes
- Inflorescence a tawny, terminal panicle; blooms July–November

ABOUT

Freshwater Marshes

Fresh-water marshes are found throughout the coastal drainage wherever fresh water accumulates. Some of the most extensive fresh-water marshes were once were found in the upper delta of San Francisco Bay; however, these have been diked for farmland with only remnants remaining.

A fresh-water marsh usually has shallow water which is often clogged with dense masses of vegetation, sedges, cattails, and rushes. Pools of water are common; however, as a marsh ages, vegetation will accumulate, often filling in all the open water, and eventually creating a meadow. Water can stand or move sluggishly.

Plants in this section include both fresh-water marsh plants and some of the more common aquatic plants found in or on the surface of open water.

Growth of fresh-water plants is generally rapid and sizable, often leading to clogged waterways. Almost all of the plants are perennials and reproduce vegetatively; that is, they spread by new plants developing from rhizomes or roots. The most impressive examples are cattails and sedges which once could be measured in terms of square miles in the Central Valley.

SPECIAL CHARACTERISTICS OF FRESH-WATER PLANTS:

- air tubes to roots
- air pockets in stems for buoyancy
- reduced outer cuticle for better oxygen and carbon dioxide exchange
- green chloroplasts (photosynthetic bodies) concentrated near upper leaf surface
- two types of leaves in amphibious plants

Fresh-water plants have some of the same adaptations as salt marsh plants which enable them to live in a watery environment, a nice example of parallel evolution. They have **air tubes to their roots**, and **air spaces in their stems** so that air can diffuse to their roots.

Floating plants have **air pockets in their stems and leaves for buoyancy**, essential to an organism dependent upon light for food production. To compensate for reduced light under water, the **stiff outer coat** (cuticle) of aquatic plants **is reduced**, enabling oxygen and carbon dioxide exchange to occur under water more easily.

In addition, **green chloroplasts** which convert light into energy for food production **are located just under the thin surface tissue for increased efficiency**. Amphibious plants such as *Ranunculus aquatica* var. *hispidulus*, have **two types of leaves**, a set of finely divided submerged leaves which have large surfaces for increased gas exchange, and a set of coarse entire leaves with leaf pores or stomata more numerous on the upper surface of floating leaves. Emergent or upright plants such as cattails, growing largely above water, are confined to the shallow margins of ponds or waterways.

HORSETAIL FAMILY *Equisetaceae*

Horsetail

Equisetum arvense

- Usually in wet places though this species will also grow in shaded dry areas throughout coastal California
- Erect, cylindrical, jointed stem overlaid with vertical rows of silica tubercles; 2-10 inches tall
- Whorled, needle-thin leaves emerging from nodes along stem
- Non-flowering plant that produces spores

BUTTERCUP FAMILY *Ranunculaceae*

Buttercup

*Ranunculus orthorhynchus var. bloomeri**

- Wet places and marshy ground along coast from Marin County north to Oregon
- Perennial with succulent stems; 6 to 20 inches tall
- Usually 3-parted leaves
- Glossy, yellow flowers; blooms May-July

* *R. muricatus* and *R. flammula* are similar species and also common in coastal wetlands.

BUTTERCUP FAMILY *Ranunculaceae*

Water Buttercup

*Ranunculus aquatilis
var. capillaceus**

- Common in permanent pools, ditches and slow streams almost throughout coastal California
- Aquatic perennial with submersed stems; 8 to 22 inches long
- Submerged leaves finely dissected
- Flower size variable, 5 small, white petals, sometimes greenish yellow at base; blooms April-July

* *R. aquatilis var. hispidulus* is the more common coastal variety. It has both floating leaves, which are simple and 3-lobed, and submerged leaves, which are finely dissected; found from Monterey County north.

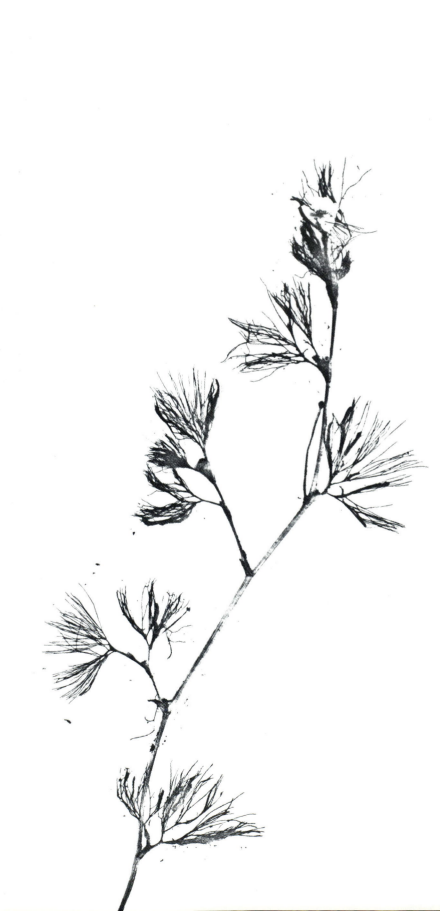

WATER-LILY FAMILY *Nymphaeaceae*

Yellow Pond-Lily

Nuphar polysepalum

- Common in freshwater ponds and slow streams from San Luis Obispo County north to Oregon
- Aquatic perennial plant
- Broad, oval leaves floating or raised above surface; 4 to 16 inches wide
- Showy, yellow flowers often raised above leaves; blooms April-September

MUSTARD FAMILY *Brassicaceae*

- Common on wet banks, bogs and springs throughout coastal California
- Perennial with prostrate or erect stems, rooting freely at nodes; 10 to 20 inches tall
- Leafy aspect to plant resulting from 3 to 11 ovate or round, paired leaflets per leaf
- Tiny, white-petaled flowers, long seed pods; blooms March-November

Water-Cress

Rorippa nasturtium-aquatica

BUCKWHEAT FAMILY *Polygonaceae*

Swamp Smartweed

Polygonum coccineum

- Occasional in low wet places, shores and margins of ponds throughout coastal California
- Perennial reproducing by seed and by long creeping, touch, horizontal rhizomes.
- Leaves broader at base and somewhat pointed at tip, 2 to 7 inches long.
- Tiny, pinkish flowers in leaf axils; blooms May-November

BUCKWHEAT FAMILY *Polygonaceae*

- Common in marshes, ponds and ditches throughout coastal California
- Aquatic to terrestrial perennial, stems swollen above nodes, erect or decumbent at base, simple or much branched; 1 to 3 feet tall

Water Smartweed, Knotweed

Polygonum punctatum

- Leaves tapering, longer than broad, and dotted
- Inconspicuous, greenish flowers on a narrow spike; blooms July-October

FIGWORT FAMILY *Scrophulariaceae*

American Brooklime

Veronica americana

- Common in freshwater marshes, along streams and near springs throughout coastal California
- Somewhat-succulent perennial with erect or decumbent stems; 4 to 40 inches tall
- Slightly toothed, oval, opposite leaves
- Violet-blue flowers in leaf axils; blooms May-August

WATER-STARWORT FAMILY *Callitrichaceae*

Water-Starwort

*Callitriche heterophylla var. bolanderi**

- Quiet water throughout coastal California
- Submerged aquatic, usually with a rosette of floating leaves at ends of very slender stems, occasionally terrestrial on margins of ponds and streams
- Leaves opposite and roundish
- Tiny flowers without petals found in leaf axils; blooms April-August

* *C. trochlearis* is found in ponds in Northern California and *C. longipedunculata* in vernal pools San Diego County to Central California

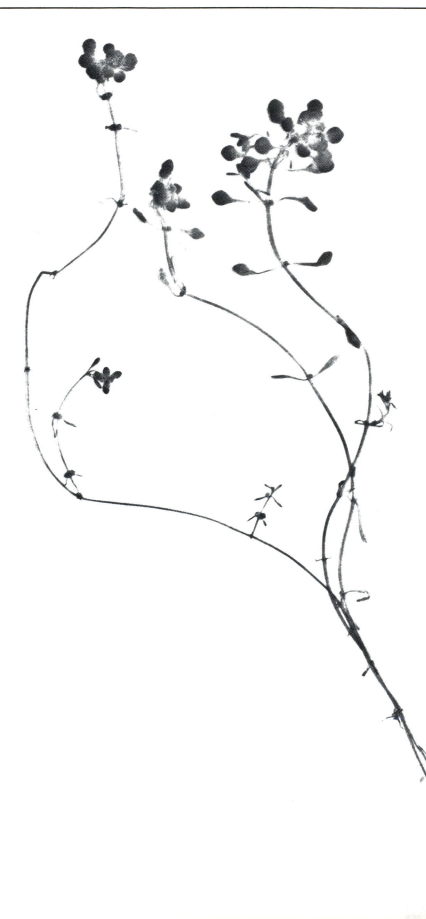

CARROT FAMILY *Apiaceae*

Marsh Pennywort

Hydrocotyle ranunculoides

- Swampy streams, shallow freshwater ponds or streams throughout coastal California
- Stems floating or creeping on mud; 2 to 4 inches long
- Lobed, circular leaves often found floating on water surface
- Tiny, white flowers in umbels often found below the surface of the water near the base of leaves; blooms March-August

WATER-PLANTAIN FAMILY *Alismataceae*

Arrowhead, Tule-potato, Wappato

*Sagittaria latifolia**

- Edge of ponds, slow streams or wet meadows throughout coastal California
- Erect perennial; 8 to 40 inches tall
- Leaves variable in size, shaped like arrowhead
- Branched inflorescence with small clusters of white-petaled flowers; blooms July-August

* A similar species, *S. cuneata*, is also found in coastal wetlands.

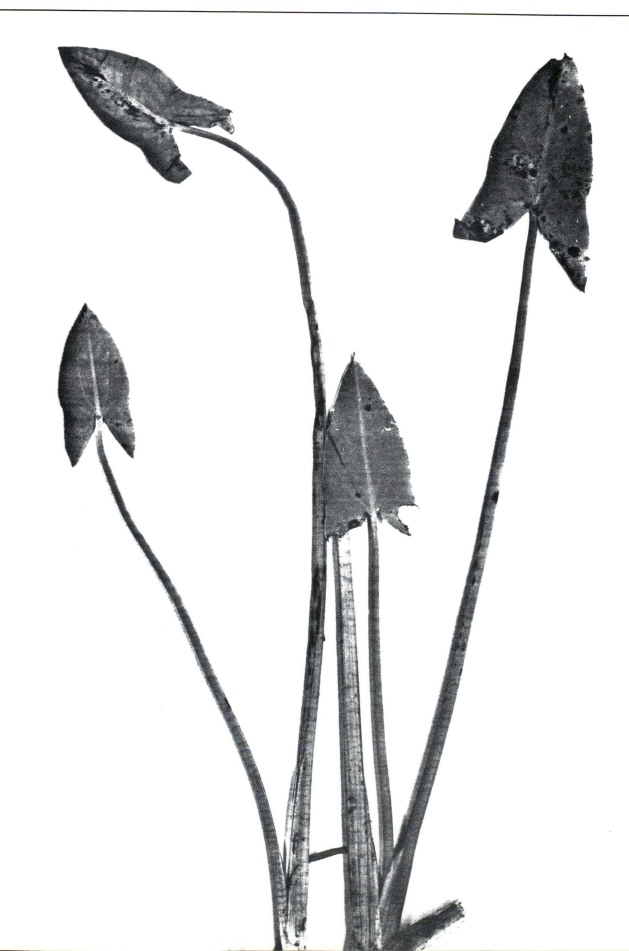

PONDWEED FAMILY *Potamogetonaceae*

Pondweed

Potamogeton foliosus *

- Ponds or slow streams throughout coastal California
- Stems flattened, leafy, slender, freely branched; 8 to 40 inches
- Leaves submerged, linear, numerous
- Flowers in short inconspicuous spikes in leaf axils; blooms July-October

* Other common species of pondweed occurring in the coastal zone are *P. pectinatus* and *P. illinoensis*.

PONDWEED FAMILY *Potamogetonaceae*

Pondweed

Potamogeton nodosus

- Common in pools and ditches from San Diego County north to Oregon
- Aquatic, floating perennial; 3 to 6 feet long
- Elliptic, leather, floating leaves
- Flowers on an inconspicuous spike; blooms May-August

CARROT FAMILY *Apiaceae*

Water Parsley

Oenanthe sarmentosa

- Common in marshes, ponds and sluggish streams, sometimes growing in massive colonies throughout coastal California
- Aquatic perennial with succulent stems, prostrate or upright growth; 1.5 to 4.5 feet tall
- Compound, pinnate, coarsely-dentate leaves
- Small, white flowers in umbels; blooms June-October

BUR-REED FAMILY *Sparganiaceae*

Bur-Reed

Sparganium eurycarpum

- Occasional in fresh or brackish marshes and along streams throughout coastal California
- Erect, stout stem, branched plant; 1.5 to 6 feet tall
- Flat leaves equaling or shorter than stem
- Branched inflorescence with round flower heads of separate male and female flowers; blooms April-August

CAT-TAIL FAMILY *Typhaceae*

Common cattail

*Typha latifolia**

- Common in freshwater marshes and marshy places throughout coastal California
- Erect, stout perennial
- Long, flat, light-green leaves
- Flowers in tall spikes with ephemeral male portion of the spike located above a thick, brown, cigar-shaped cluster of female flowers; blooms June-July

* Other species of *Typha* found in the coastal zone include: *T. domingensis, T. angustifolia* (narrow-leaved cat-tail), *T. glauca* (in S.F. Bay region) and various hybrid crosses.

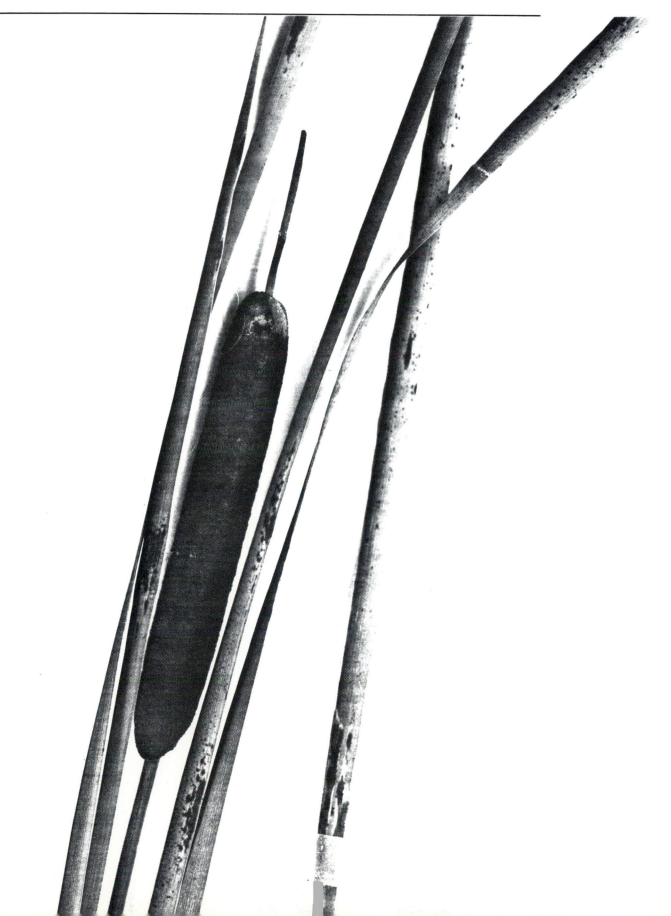

RUSH FAMILY *Juncaeae*

- Widespread in coastal swamps, meadows, dunes and marshes from Los Angeles County north to Oregon
- Creeping, erect perennial with stout rootstocks; 4 to 15 inches tall
- Flattened stems and leaves
- Dense heads of tiny, dark, reddish-brown flowers; blooms May-June

Rush

*Juncus phaeocephalus**

* The genus *Juncus*, commonly called Rush or Wire Grass, is a large group of over 200 species distributed world-wide, with 49 species found throughout California and 21 in coastal California. Rushes are usually found in moist places growing with grasses and sedges.

SEDGE FAMILY *Cyperaceae*

- Occasional along streams and springs throughout coastal California
- Perennial with stout, almost-round, erect stems; 2½ to 5½ feet tall
- Flat, broad leaves growing along stem
- Inflorescence a loose, spreading, compound umbel of spikelets with green to brown scales; blooms May-August

Scirpus or Bulrush

*Scirpus microcarpus**

* The genus *Scirpus*, commonly called Bulrush or Tule, is in the Sedge family and is a large genus of over 200 species distributed world-wide with 17 species found throughout California and 9 in coastal California.

SEDGE FAMILY *Cyperaceae*

Common Spike-Rush

Eleocharis macrostachya
(Heleocharis palustris)

- Common and widespread in marshes and vernal pools throughout coastal California
- Perennial sedge with long creeping rhizomes growing singly or in dense clumps with round or oval erect stems; 1 to 3 feet tall
- Leaves reduced to basal sheaths
- A terminal spike of inconspicuous, scale-like flowers; blooms May-August

SEDGE FAMILY *Cyperaceae*

- Common in marshes and wet meadows near the coast from San Luis Obispo County to Oregon
- Grows in large clumps with sharply triangular stems; 1 to 5 feet tall
- Leaf blades channeled above and keeled toward base
- Flowers arranged in spikes; the upper 2 or 3 spikes are male; middle spikes part male/part female and often drooping; the lower spikes are female and are erect, spreading or strongly drooping
- * The genus *Carex*, in the Sedge Family, is one of the largest genera of plants in the world with more than 1,000 species found world-wide, 144 species found in California and 45 in the wetlands of California. Identification generally requires microscopic examination. A large and a small species are shown in this book.

Slough Sedge

Carex obnupta*

SEDGE FAMILY *Cyperaceae*

- Occasional in moist soils west of the coastal ranges from Santa Cruz to Del Norte counties
- Grows in loose clumps with slender stems and leaves; 8 to 22 inches tall
- Leaves flat or with margins somewhat rolled back
- Flowers arranged in small spikes

* This species is similar to *C. bolanderi* which is somewhat more common.

† The genus *Carex*, in the Sedge Family, is one of the largest genera of plants in the world with more than 1,000 species found world-wide, 144 species found in California and 45 in the wetlands of California. Identification generally requires microscopic examination. A large and a small species are shown in this book.

Sedge

Carex leptopoda* †

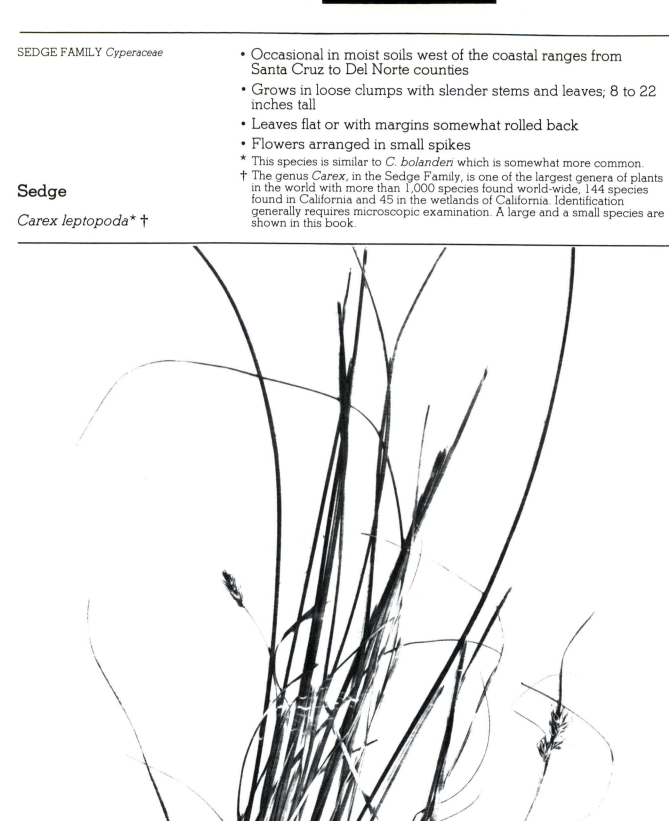

GRASS FAMILY *Poaceae*

Mannagrass

Glyceria occidentalis

- Swampy shallow-water places, ditches and fresh water marshes; Marin County north to Oregon
- Culms soft, ascending from a decumbent rooting base, 24-48 inches tall
- Leaf blades $^1/_{10}$ to $^6/_{10}$ inches wide
- Inflorescence a 12 to 20 inch panicle with $^1/_2$ to 1 inch spikelets; blooms June-August

GRASS FAMILY *Poaceae*

Weak Mannagrass

Torreyochloa pallida var. *pauci-flora (Puccinella pauciflora)*

- Shallow water pools or wet banks; San Mateo County north
- Decumbent rooting base (rhizomes) with culms 20 to 50 inches tall
- leaf blades flat, $1/5$ to $7/10$ inches wide
- Inflorescence a panicle 4 to 8 inches long with 5-6 flowered spikelets, often purplish; blooms July-September

ABOUT

Riparian Woodlands

The types of vegetation common to a riparian habitat include trees, shrubs and herbs that are restricted to the banks of lakes, perennial and intermittent streams and rivers.

Riparian plants are often strikingly different from the vegetation found at the top of a stream bank. In the north, where rainfall is high and vegetation more lush, differences between a riparian forest and an adjacent upland forest are sometimes not obvious. In forested areas the overstory may be similar to the adjacent forest but the understory will contain a variety of plant species adapted to a moist or wet substrate, such as salmonberry, willow, twinberry and lady fern.

Typically, riparian habitat is supplied with water from a remote source (a drainage basin, aquifer or watercourse); it has high soil moisture and even occasional seasonal flooding; and it is linear, usually extending in discontinuous patterns. One edge of riparian habitat is a freshwater body (a stream, river, marsh or lake) and the other an adjacent upland where soil moisture may be sharply reduced. While most riparian woodlands have been destroyed, remnants do exist throughout the state though most are significantly degraded.

Vast riparian forests once surrounded the sacramento drainage across the Central Valley, and other river systems in California. Clearing for agriculture, timber harvesting, groundwater pumping and water diversion have all resulted in the destruction of all but remnants of riparian habitat throughout California. In many places just a few alder trees or a cottonwood tree is all that remains of a riparian plant assemblage.

Even so, important examples of this wetland habitat type are found throughout Coastal California. In Northern California remnants are found in broad floodplains, abandoned river channels and the bottoms adjacent to channels. In Southern California riparian vegetation occurs in a narrow band along streams and rivers. The size of trees that have access to water easily distinguishes them from the sparse vegetation of adjacent arid soils.

SPECIAL CHARACTERISTICS OF RIPARIAN PLANTS

- large size of trees
- deciduous vegetation
- leaves usually large and relatively soft

Because of the potential for year-around moisture and deeper river bottom soils, **riparian trees often grow to great size**. Big leaf maple (*Acer macrophyllulm*), western cottonwood, (*Populus fremontii)*, and western sycamore, (*Platanus racemosa)* all grow to over 30 feet and provide one of the few links between the flora of California and that found East of the Rockies. **Riparian trees and most riparian shrubs are deciduous**; that is, they lose their leaves annually. Stream and river bottoms are cold in the winter, so there is no advantage to retaining leaves and, since there is moisture available over long periods of time, leaf production and food storage can occur more leisurely over a longer period. In general, **leaves are large, open and relatively soft**, again indicating adequate water supply and some competition for light in the riparian thickets that form around streams.

BRACKEN FAMILY *Dennstaediaceae*

Bracken Fern

*Pteridium aquilinum
var. pubescens*

- Widely distributed in the coastal strand throughout California
- Coarse, branched fern growing erect or reclining; 1 to 4½ feet tall
- Three-times pinnate blades with felt-like covering near the base
- Non-flowering plant producing spores

WOOD FERN FAMILY *Dryopteridiaceae*

Lady Fern

Athyrium filix-femina
var. *cyclogorum*

- Bogs and marshes along the coast from Santa Barbara County north into Oregon
- Erect, arching fronds with 2-3 pinnate blades; 2-3 feet tall
- non-flowering spore producing plant

LAUREL FAMILY *Lauraceae*

California Bay

Umbellularia californica

- Often a riparian tree from San Diego County north in the Coast Ranges into Oregon
- Evergreen tree with broad crown; 30 to 100 feet tall
- Aromatic, shiny, pointed, narrow leaves
- Yellow-green, inconspicuous flowers which produce purple, ovoid, stone-centered fruit; blooms December-May

SAXIFRAGE FAMILY *Saxifragaceae*

Canyon Gooseberry

Ribes menziesii var. leptosmum

- Occasional in canyons and flats of outer Coast Ranges from San Luis Obispo County into Oregon
- Loosely branched shrub; 3 to 6 feet tall
- Leaves rounded in outline, velvety above with gland-tipped hairs beneath
- Purplish flowers producing a densely bristled berry; blooms March-April

ROSE FAMILY *Rosaceae*

- Woods and damp places in coastal strand from San Luis Obispo County to Mendocino County.
- Green mound builder or trailer or partial climber, the long running stems tip-rooting with straightish bristle-prickles
- Thin, smooth, toothed leaves in groups of 3

California Blackberry

Rubus vitifolius
Rubus ursinus (*R. vitifolius*)

- Male and female flowers, both white, are found on separate plants, the male flowers generally twice the size of the female. Flowers are arranged in clusters that develop into black edible berries; blooms March-July

ROSE FAMILY *Rosaceae*

Salmonberry

Rubus spectabilis

- Occasional in well-watered canyons or in brush thickets in wet soil near the coast from Marin County into Oregon
- Branching, glandless, leafy shrub; sterile shoots sparingly covered with prickles; 6 to 14 feet
- Leaves with 3 thin, double-toothed, ovate leaflets
- Red to salmon-color flowers; fruit a salmon to yellow-colored, edible berry; blooms March-June

SYCAMORE FAMILY *Platanaceae*

Sycamore

Platanus racemosa

- Along stream beds and water courses of South Coast Ranges into Mexico
- Large trees with thin scaling bark on ashy, white trunks and limbs; 30-80 feet tall
- Large deciduous 5-lobed leaves
- Flowers minute, fruit a dense bristly head; blooms February-April

BIRCH FAMILY *Betulaceae*

Red Alder

Alnus oregona

- Stream banks and marshy places along the coast from Santa Cruz County to Del Norte County
- Tall trees, or where exposed to wind and sun can be reduced to shrub size; thin pale grey or whitish bark; up to 80 feet tall
- Oval pointed leaves with toothy edges
- Male flowers in 4-6 inch catkins, female in small ½ inch cones; blooms March-April

WAX-MYRTLE FAMILY *Myricaceae*

Wax-Myrtle

Myrica calitornica

- Occasional in bogs, swamps and along stream courses throughout coastal California
- Small tree or shrub with thin, dark-gray, smooth bark; 6 to 30 feet tall
- Alternate dark-green, glossy, long, thin, pointed leaves
- Male and female flowers in short catkins in leaf axils; fruit covered with a whitish wax; blooms March-April

WALNUT FAMILY *Juglandaceae*

Black Walnut

Juglans californica

- Locally common along river courses below 2,500 feet; Ventura to Orange and San Bernardino counties
- Low tree with several trunks; 10 to 30 feet tall
- Leaves with pinnately-paired, pointed leaflets
- Male flowers in a 2-3 inch catkin, inconspicuous female flowers at ends of growing shoots produce edible nuts; blooms April-May

WILLOW FAMILY *Salicaceae*

- Common in swamps and along stream banks in Central and Southern California
- Spreading tree; up to 100 feet
- Smooth, toothy, triangular, shiny, yellow-green leaves with flat stems; yellow in fall

Cottonwood

Populus fremontii

- Separate male and female trees each producing catkins, those on the female trees producing minute, cottony seeds with fine, silky hairs; blooms March-April

WILLOW FAMILY *Salicaceae*

Yellow Willow

Salix lasiandra

- Swamps and stream courses throughout coastal California
- Conspicuously yellow to red twigs, tree-like growth habit; 20 to 50 feet tall
- Leaves dark-green shining above with characteristic wart-like glands on leaf stems
- ¾ to 2½ inch catkins on male trees, 1 to 4 inch catkins on female trees; blooms March-May

WILLOW FAMILY *Salicaceae*

Sandbar Willow

Salix hindsiana

- Common along ditches, sloughs and sandbars throughout coastal California
- Young twigs grey and covered with short dense matted woolly hairs, shrub or treelike growth; 6 to 24 feet tall
- Narrow, linear leaves, grayish in appearance
- ¾ to 2 inch catkins on leafy stalks on separate male and female trees; blooms March–May

WILLOW FAMILY *Salicaceae*

Arroyo Willow

Salix lasiolepis *

- Common along stream banks and wet places throughout coastal California
- Grows in dense patches as shrubs or as trees; 6 to 50 feet tall
- Narrow pointed leaves
- Separate male and female trees, each produce ¾ to 2 inch catkins; blooms March-May

* There are 13 species of willow growing in coastal California. According to Mason, Arroyo Willow is the most common thicket willow.

MAPLE FAMILY *Aceraceae*

Big-Leaf Maple

Acer macrophyllum

- Common on stream banks throughout coastal California
- Deciduous round-topped tree; 15-100 feet tall
- Leaves 3-5 parted, few-toothed, and coarsely, irregularly lobed
- Clusters of greenish flowers developing into winged fruits; blooms April-May

MAPLE FAMILY *Aceraceae*

Box Elder

Acer negundo. ssp. californicum

- Along streams and wet meadows, coast ranges from Santa Barbara County north
- Round-headed tree often with several stems; 20 to 50 feet tall
- Leaves densely fuzzy on underside, pinnately 3-parted with terminal leaflet, lobed and ovate
- Small greenish flowers; winged fruit; blooms March-April

HONEYSUCKLE FAMILY *Caprifoliaceae*

Twinberry

Lonicera involucrata
var. ledebourii

- Occasional along streams from Santa Barbara County to Humboldt County
- Upright shrub; 3 to 10 feet high
- Oval, pointed leaves shed in winter
- Yellow, paired flowers tinged with red; fruit a black, ovoid, double berry; blooms March-April

ABOUT

Vernal Pools

A vernal pool is a small depression that fills with water during the winter and supports a unique assemblage of plants. Vernal pools are underlain with a dense claypan or hardpan soil which has formed over the last half-million years. These soil formations, common on the coastal terraces of California, are among the state's oldest soils. The hardpans are so thick and densely cemented that water cannot seep away into the lower soil column and, instead, accumulates above the hardpan to evaporate away in the spring. Hogwallows, a name often used interchangeably with vernal pools, differ only in that they contain a lesser amount of standing water.

As vernal pools dry up in the spring, various plants flower, often in conspicuous rings of color. The boundary between a vernal pool and a surrounding upland grassland is usually quite distinct particularly when the flowers are in bloom. During the summer and fall the boundary between a dried vernal pool and an upland is far more difficult to determine — another job for the expert.

Over half of the plants found in vernal pools in California are found only in California. Made rare by the extensive urbanization and spread of agriculture which has occurred over the past 30 years, several species today have populations occurring in only one or two locations. Their disappearance would result in the loss of unique combinations of genes that have evolved in a specialized type of habitat in the ecologically unique island of California, isolated by the Sierra on the east and the Pacific on the west.

Vernal pools are found in few places in the world outside California, in fact only in southern Oregon and in the Cape Province of South Africa. A certain combination of climate, topography and soil development is necessary for vernal pool formation.

The major vernal pools of the coastal area of California occur in the San Diego coastal terraces. Other important vernal pools are found on the Santa Rose Plateau in Riverside County and throughout the great Central Valley of California, particularly on the eastern side. Vernal ponds and vernal lakes, which differ in size, occur in San Luis Obispo County. Small and less significant vernal pools, some only a few square feet, can be found on terraces above the Pacific Ocean all along the coast into Northern California, wherever impervious clay soils exist. The Nature Conservancy is protecting some of the most significant pools by purchasing them with private donations.

SPECIAL CHARACTERISTICS OF VERNAL POOLS:

- annual plants more common than perennial plants
- annual plants survive dry periods as seeds
- no shrubs or trees occur in vernal pools

Water depth, frequency and duration of flooding and the effects of competition determine the success of a plant species in a given year in a vernal pool. Soil characteristics (pH and clay content) also affect species distribution. **Wet periods alternating with long periods of desiccation have favored annual plants over perennial plants. Annuals survive long dry summer and fall periods as seeds.** When moisture comes, seeds germinate quickly, establish small root systems. The annuals bloom early and set their seeds before moisture has evaporated. The energy of the plant is directed towards rapid seed production, assuring special continuity in a harsh environment. Over 70 percent of the plants of vernal pools are native annuals, many of them very small. Some create showy rings of color along the edges of ponded water as it evaporates. **There are no shrubs or trees in vernal pools.**

QUILLWORT FAMILY *Isoetaceae*

- Occasional along margins of ponds or streams or on wet soil on mesas of San Diego throughout coastal California
- Small, erect aquatic or terrestrial plants growing from underground corms*; 1 to 8 inches tall

Quillwort

- Quill-like leaves
- Non-flowering plant producing spores

Isoetes nuttallii

* A separated corm is shown in photocopy.

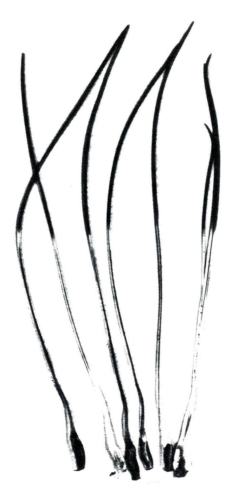

FALSE MERMAID FAMILY *Limnanthaceae*

Meadow-Foam

Limnanthes douglasii
var. douglasii

- Vernal pools and wet meadows in coastal zone of Central and Northern California
- Annual plants usually growing in large patches, spectacular when in bloom
- Pinnately divided, usually toothed, soft leaves
- Showy yellow petals with white tips; blooms March-May

PHLOX FAMILY *Polemoniaceae*

Skunkweed

Navarretia bakeri*

- Vernal pools of coastal Northern California
- Erect much-branched annual having a distinctive odor; 1 to 5 inches tall
- Hairy, linear to linear dissected leaves
- Tiny white flowers clustered in heads; blooms May-June

* A similar but more prostrate form, *Navarretia prostrata*, is more commonly found in vernal pools of coastal Southern California.

BORAGE FAMILY *Boraginaceae*

- Moist clay or beds of vernal pools of San Diego County mesas
- Stems slender and hairy, usually branched below, spreading or erect; 4 to 15 inches
- Smallish, linear to oval leaves
- Tiny, white flowers in an uncoiling inflorescence; blooms March-May

Popcorn Flower

Plagiobothrys acanthocarpus*

* Distinguished from the genus *Cryptantha* largely by microscopic examination of seed-containing nutlets

FIGWORT FAMILY *Scrophulariaceae*

Mudwort

Limosella acaulis

- Wet, muddy places; Marin County south
- Mat-forming tufts or clumps of rosette plants
- Leaf blades flat spoon shaped, long petioles, $1/2$ to 2 inches long
- Tiny white to lavender, solitary flowers; blooms May-October

MINT FAMILY *Lamiaceae*

Vernal Pool Mint

*Pogogyne zizyphoroides**

- Occasional in vernal pools of Santa Clara County to Humboldt County
- Small, erect, aromatic annual; 2 to 12 inches tall
- Ovate, aromatic, opposite leaves
- Tiny, lavender, tubular flowers clustered in axils of bracts; blooms March-May

* *P. abramsii* and *P. nudiuscula* are also found on coastal mesas of San Diego County

STONECROP FAMILY *Crassulaceae*

Tillaea, Pigmy-Weed

Crassula aquatica
(Tillaea aquatica)

- Occasional on drying mud flats and vernal pools in coastal California
- Diminutive annual with spreading or decumbent stems becoming reddish with age and drying; ¾ to 2½ inches tall
- Minute, opposite, oblong, fleshy leaves
- Tiny, greenish-white flowers in leaf axils; blooms March-July

LOOSESTRIFE FAMILY *Lythraceae*

Loosestrife

Lythrum hyssopifolium

- Widespread in moist places in marches and at the margins of streams and pools throughout coastal California
- Annual or short-lived perennial, simple or branches, erect or prostrate; 4 to 40 inches
- Linear to oblong leaves
- Pale pink to lavender flowers in leaf axils; blooms April-October

BELL-FLOWER FAMILY *Campanulaceae*

Downingia

`Downingia concolor*`

- In vernal pools of coast ranges of California
- Low, soft-stemmed annual; 2 to 8 inches
- Small, tender, alternate leaves
- Purple spot on base of an enlarged lower lip of a blue and white, irregular flower; blooms April-July

* *D. pulchella* and *D. cuspidata* are also found in coastal vernal pools.

CARROT FAMILY *Apiaceae*

Button Snakeroot or Button Celery

Eryngium armatum*

- In vernal pools and near coast from Santa Barbara County north to Humboldt County
- Branched stems growing prostrate to ascending; 2 to 26 inches tall
- Spiny toothed leaves
- Minute, white-petaled flowers in heads at ends of branches; blooms May-August

* A similar plant, *Eryngium aristulatum* is found in coastal salt marshes, Ventura to Humboldt counties.

SUNFLOWER FAMILY *Asteraceae*

Woolly Marbles

Psilocarphus tenellus

- Dried beds of vernal pools in coastal California
- Inconspicuous, woolly, usually prostrate, branching annual; up to 4 inches
- Opposite, woolly leaves that cluster around flower heads
- Inconspicuous flowers clustered in terminal heads; blooms April-June

FLOWERING QUILLWORT FAMILY *Lilaeaceae*

Flowering Quillwort

Lilaea scilloides

- In fresh or brackish, muddy and marshy places throughout coastal California
- Aquatic annual, 2-8 inches tall
- Tufted, fleshy, linear leaves with a sheathing base
- Two kinds of inflorescence: one, basal in axils of leaves; other, at water level a short, dense, erect spike borne on slender flower stalk; blooms March-October

LILY FAMILY *Liliaceae*

White brodiaea

Triteleia hyacinthina

- Common in low moist meadows, vernal pools, and along streams in coastal California
- Erect, perennial spring wildflower with underground corm; 12 to 24 inches tall
- Few, grass-like leaves
- White, bowl-shaped flowers arranged in an umbel with green midvein on each segment; blooms April-June

GRASS FAMILY *Poaceae*

Orcutt-Grass

Orcuttia california

- Vernal pools and mudflats in coastal Los Angeles and Riverside counties
- Low annual grass; 2 to 11 inches tall
- Short leaf blades
- Inflorescence a spike of rather large spikelets; blooms May-June

GRASS FAMILY *Poaceae*

Hair Grass

Deschampsia danthonoides

- Common in low scattered drying vernal pools and wet meadows throughout coastal California
- Annual grass, 4 to 20 inches tall
- Few, very-fine leaf blades
- Inflorescence a fine, purple-tipped panicle; blooms March-April

GRASS FAMILY *Poaceae*

Meadow Foxtail

Alopecurus saccatus

- Occasional in wet places in coast ranges from San Diego County to Oregon
- Erect, annual grass; 6 to 12 inches tall
- Inflated sheath and flat leaf blades
- Soft, dense, spike-like flower head; blooms March-June

GLOSSARY

annual—a plant which completes its life within a year.

bract—a reduced or modified leaf, particularly the scale-like leaves in a flower cluster.

catkin—a deciduous spike or spike-like inflorescence of unisexual, apetalous flowers.*(Figure 1)*

compound—a leaf separated into two or more distinct leaflets or several parts united into a common whole as in a compound flower, a daisy-like flower.

corm—a bulb-like stem usually found underground.

deciduous—losing leaves seasonally.

decumbent—reclining on the ground but with the end ascending.

dentate—marginal teeth which point outward.

exfoliating—peeling off in thin layers.

head—compact group of flowers that occur together and form a circular cluster at the end of a stem or branch. *(Figure 1)*

herbaceous—pertaining to a plant without a persistent woody stem that dies to the ground each year.

inflorescence—the arrangement of flower-clusters on a floral axis.

leaf axil—the upper angle between a leaf and a stem.

panicle—a compound inflorescence branching from a central axis. *(Figure 1)*

perennial—a plant lasting for 3 years or more.

pinnate—a compound leaf with paired leaflets on opposite sides of an elongated axis.

raceme—an inflorescence with a single axis, the flowers arranged on simple stalks. *(Figure 1)*

rhizome—a horizontal underground stem.

riparian habitat[1]—an environment with an association of plant species growing adjacent to fresh-water water courses, including perennial and intermittent streams, lakes, and other bodies of fresh water.

sheath—a tubular basal part of a leaf that wraps around a stem.

spike—a type of inflorescence with numerous stemless flowers growing directly from an elongated axis. *(Figure 1)*

spikelets—the segment of a grass inflorescence surrounded by a pair of bracts.

stigma—the pollen-receiving part of a female flower.

umbel—inflorescence of few to many flowers on stalks of approximately equal length arising from the top of a flower stem. *(Figure 1)*

vernal pool—a small depression, usually underlain by some sub-surface layer which prohibits drainage into the lower soils profile, in which, during the rainy reason, water may stand for periods of time sufficient to prohibit zonal vegetation from developing. The habitat is intermediate in duration of inundation between marshes (never or only rarely dry) and most zonal communities (never or only rarely submerged).[1]

coastal wetlands—lands within the coastal zone which may be covered periodically or permanently with shallow water and include salt water marshes, freshwater marshes, open or closed brackish-water marshes, swamps, mudflats and fens. *(See Appendix 1)*[1]

[1] Statewide Interpretive Guideline for Wetlands and Other Wet Environmentally Sensitive Habitat Areas, February 4, 1981.

FIGURE 1

Raceme

Head

Umbel

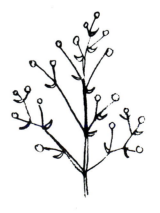

Panicle

Spike

BIBLIOGRAPHY

1. Atwater, B. F., S. G. Conard, J. N. Dowden, C. W. Hedel, R. L. Macdonald, W. Savage. 1979. "History, Landforms, and Vegetation of the Estuary's Tidal Marshes," Pp. 347-385. In Conomos, T. J. (ed.), *San Francisco Bay: the Urbanized Estuary*. Pacific Division of the American Association for the Advancement of Science, San Francisco.

2. Clark, J. 1974. *Coastal Ecosystems*. Conservation Foundation, Washington, D.C.

3. Clark, J. 1980. *California Coastal Catalogue*. The American Littoral Society, New Jersey.

4. Faber, P. 1980. *Report on the Current Status of the Muzzi Marsh Prepared for the Golden Gate Bridge, Highway and Transportation District*, San Francisco, California.

5. Hickman, J. (Ed.). 1993. *A Jepson Manual: Higher Plants of California*. University of California, Berkeley.

6. Holland, R. and F. T. Griggs. 1976. *A Unique Habitat—California's Vernal Pools*. Fremontia 4(3):3-6.

7. Holland, R. and S. Jain. 1977. "Vernal Pools," pp. 515-533. In M. G. Barbour and J. Major. *Terrestrial Vegetation of California*. John Wiley and Sons, New York.

8. Howell, J. T. 1970. *Marin Flora*. University of California Press, Berkeley.

9. Macdonald, K. 1977. "Coastal Salt Marsh," pp. 262-294. In M. G. Barbour and J. Major, (eds.) *Terrestrial Vegetation of California*. John Wiley & Sons, New York.

10. Mason, H. L. 1969. *A Flora of the Marshes of California*. University of California Press, Berkeley.

11. Munz, P. A. and D. D. Keck. 1973. *A California Flora*. University of California Press, Berkeley.

12. Reimond, R. J. and W. H. Queen. 1974. *Ecology of Halophytes*. Academic Press, New York.

13. Teal, J. and M. 1969. *Life and Death of the Salt Marsh*. Audubon/Ballantine, New York.

14. Zedler, J., T. Winfield and D. Mauriello. 1978. "Primary Productivity in a Southern California Estuary." *Coastal Zone '78*, Vol II: 649-662. American Society of Civil Engineers, New York.

INDEX

Since 1987, the California Department of Fish and Game (CDFG) has used the wetland definition provided by the U.S. Fish and Wildlife Service (USFWS) and supported in the 1987 Corps of Engineers Wetlands Delineation Manual. This definition utilizes hydric soils, saturation or inundation, and vegetation as its three criteria for wetland delineation. The difference between the USFWS and CDFG approaches to delineation centers on the fact that USFWS will consider an area a wetland if at least one of these criteria is met, and CDFG requires the presence of all three criteria before considering an area a wetland.

The specific USFWS definition follows:

"Wetlands are lands tranitional between terrestrial and aquatic systems where the water table is usually at or near the surface or the land is covered by shallow water. For purposes of this classification, wetlands must have one or more of the following three attributes: (1) at least periodically, the land supports a predominance of hydrophytes, (2) the substrate is predominantly undrained hydric soil; and (3) the substrate is non-soil and is saturated with water or covered by shallow water at some time during the growing season of each year." (*Classification of Wetlands and Deepwater Habitats of the United States*; FWS/OBS 79/31; December, 1979).

In 1993, Congress requested that the National Academy of Sciences, through a committee formed by the National Research Council, provide an assessment of the adequacy of wetland definitions, a basis for applying definitions through delineation manuals, an overview of present knowledge regarding the structure and function of wetlands, and a sense of regional variation among wetlands. This report recommends that a new federal delineation manual should be prepared — to update the 1987 Corps Manual which essentially contained the USFWS wetland definition shown above — for common use by all federal agencies involved in the regulation of wetlands. The report also recommends a "reference" or non-regulatory definition of wetlands to be the heart of future delineation efforts. The definition suggested in the report follows:

"A wetland is an ecosystem that depends on constant or recurrent shallow inundation or saturation at or near the surface of the substrate. The minimum essential characteristics of a wetland are recurrent, sustained inundation or saturation at or near the surface and the presence of physical, chemical, and biological features reflective of recurrent, sustained inundation or saturation. Common diagnostic features of wetlands are hydric soils and hydrophytic vegetation. These features will be present except where specific physiochemical, biotic, or anthropogenic factors have removed them or prevented their development" (Wetlands: Characteristics and Boundaries; National Academy of Sciences Report, 1995).

Though this NAS definition focuses on three major factors to characterize a wetland — water, substrate, and vegetation — the report states that it is often scientifically defensible to infer information about one factor from another, thus supporting the USFWS standing policy. The specific criteria for each of these factors is summarized below:

Water: the report recommends the threshold for duration of saturation as 14 days during the growing season in most years (over 50%), the depth of saturation is estimated as 1 ft. (30 cm.), and in both estimations the local or regional water table depth and hydrology should be taken into account.

Substrate: the hydric soils should be defined according to the Natural Resource Conservation Service (formerly the Soil Conservation Service) who has developed a national hydric soils list entitled "Hydric Soils of the United States." The report suggests that this list should be updated, but that it is generally valid.

Vegetation: The NRCS also publishes a "National List of Plant Species that Occur in Wetlands." Again, this list should be updated but is currently scientifically credible. The report notes that either a dominance measure (the 50% rule) or a prevalence index can be used to quantify the predominance of hydrophytic vegetation but stresses that either of these indicators are not meaningful in the absence of information on soils, hydrology, or both.

On August 24th, 1993, the Clinton Administration released a new wetlands policy ("Protecting America's Wetlands: A Fair, Flexible, and Effective Approach"). This policy furthered the commitment recommended in a National Wetlands Policy Forum of 1987 and echoed during the Bush Administration for "no net loss of wetlands." The Clinton wetlands policy document was accompanied by a final regulation issued jointly by the U.S. Army Corps of Engineers and Environmental Protection Agency ensuring that "approximately 53 million acres of prior converted cropland — areas which no longer exhibit wetland characteristics — will not be subject to wetlands regulations." This regulatory change removed many areas of controversy on private lands from wetland delineation squabbles, but the controversy no doubt will continue until a new delineation manual is developed.

ABOUT THE AUTHOR

Phyllis M. Faber lives in Mill Valley, near the edge of San Francisco Bay. As a biologist, she has spent many years exploring the salt marshes of the bay and teaching classes in marsh ecology to high school, college and adult students. Following an active role supporting the 1972 passage of Proposition 20, which created the California Coastal Act of 1972, Faber served as a commissioner on the California Coastal Commission for seven years. She has been involved in numerous wetland restoration projects in San Francisco Bay and currently is carrying out a long-term monitoring program for several marshes around the bay. Ms. Faber has been editor of *Fremontia*, the Journal of the California Native Plant Society, since 1984, and is director of publications for the Society.